LIVING
YOUR
PURPOSE
journal

THIS JOURNAL BELONGS TO

_____

Published in the United States by: Hay House, Inc.: www.hayhouse.com®
Published in Australia by: Hay House Australia Pty. Ltd.: www.hayhouse.com.au
Published in the United Kingdom by: Hay House UK, Ltd.: www.hayhouse.co.uk
Published in India by: Hay House Publishers India: www.hayhouse.co.in

Cover and interior design: Karla Baker

Tradepaper ISBN: 978-1-4019-6688-1

10 9 8 7 6 5 4 3 2 1
1st edition, December 2021
Printed in the United States of America

LIVING YOUR PURPOSE
journal

A GUIDED PATH TO FINDING
SUCCESS AND INNER PEACE

DR. WAYNE W. DYER

HAY HOUSE, INC.
Carlsbad, California · New York City
London · Sydney · New Delhi

INTRODUCTION

Wayne Dyer was an incredible writer, but he never stopped being a teacher as well—forever leading by example, and excited to share any insights he had or discoveries he made with the rest of us. We are so grateful that we can still hear him through his many books, lectures, and videos, as his words resonate now more than they ever have. That brings us to this journal, which includes some of his writings on living a genuinely successful and peaceful life, which Wayne certainly had.

As the father of eight, he once said that he most wanted his children "to value themselves, to become risk takers, to be self-reliant, to be free from stress and anxiety, to be able to celebrate their present moments, to experience a lifetime of wellness, to fulfill their own spiritual callings, to be creative—and, most significantly, to live with a sense of inner peace, regardless of any and all external circumstances." We feel that each and every one of us would benefit from this type of life, one in which we have the courage to listen to the voice of our soul, choose love over fear, and do what we were put on this earth to do.

We hope this journal will help you fulfill the purpose of your life. And don't worry if you don't know what that purpose is, as there are many exercises to help you find it out, remove blocks to it, and manifest the Divine and practical support you need to fulfill it. You'll also find inspirational quotes from Wayne and others that we hope encourage you. As he said in his movie *The Shift*, "When you get it—that you don't do things because of what somebody else is going to do for you, but you do them because you're living your life's purpose—you can light up the whole world with that kind of love. That's how it works for me."

May this book do the same for you.

The Editors at Hay House

Success and inner peace are your birthright. You are a child of God— and as such, you're entitled to a life of joy, love, and happiness.

AS WE BEGIN, IT'S VITALLY IMPORTANT THAT YOU GET THIS MESSAGE:

You are not your body, nor are you your personality or any of your possessions or accomplishments. You are the beloved. A miracle. A part of the eternal perfection. A piece of the Divine intelligence that supports everything and everyone on this planet. You have come to this earth for a brief moment in eternity for a reason. And staying aligned with what feels like your purpose is the key to living a fully functioning life, day in and day out.

"How can I find my purpose?" is one of the questions that I am asked most often. That's what this journal is for. In it, I share words of wisdom that have helped me and countless others, as well as a number of exercises to help you actively tune in to the voice of your true self. I use the word *actively* here on purpose, as action is critical for ensuring that what is in your mind shows up in your life. I also encourage you to use your creativity as much as you'd like throughout. There are lots of writing exercises, but if you are a more visual person, there are many opportunities for you to draw or paste collages in these pages as well. (There are extra pages in the back of the journal if you need more room to express yourself for any of the entries.) However you want to do the exercises, just be sure to take the time necessary to complete them—there is no timetable for this journey.

Note that we will be using affirmations throuthought the journal, which are powerful statements to help you manifest your dreams into reality. I will also reference a higher power here, which is called God, Spirit, the Source, the Divine, the Tao, or the Universe—it does not matter what you choose to call it, nor do you need to be religious to find and live your purpose.

Hopefully, when we ultimately reach the end of the book, you will feel how miraculous you are and feel ready to accept the success and inner peace that is your birthright.

I BELIEVE WE ALL COME TO THIS WORLD WITH MUSIC INSIDE US, WHICH WE ARE MEANT TO PLAY NO MATTER WHAT. WE MIGHT TRY TO IGNORE IT, BUT SOONER OR LATER WE NEED TO PLAY THAT MUSIC IF WE ARE MEANT TO ENJOY A LIFE OF SUCCESS AND INNER PEACE.

There's a silent something within that intends you to express yourself. That something is your soul telling you to listen, and it will never leave you alone. You may try to disregard it or pretend it doesn't exist, but in honest moments of contemplative communion with yourself, you'll sense the emptiness waiting for you to fill it with your music. It wants you to take the risks involved, and to ignore your ego and the egos of others who tell you that an easier, safer, or more secure path is best for you.

You may indeed find yourself living a comfortable life when you don't follow your instincts. You pay your bills, fill out all the right forms, and live a life of fitting in and doing things by the book. But it's a book that was written by somebody else. It's time to change that.

What is your passion? What stirs your soul and makes you feel like you're totally in harmony with why you showed up here in the first place? Write down anything that comes to mind here.

IF YOU'RE STRUGGLING TO COME UP WITH ANYTHING YOU'RE PASSIONATE ABOUT, LET'S GO BACK TO YOUR CHILDHOOD.

Is there an item that represents an early call of your soul: maybe a short story you wrote, a picture you painted, a scouting badge, or an award for service? Did a teacher give you encouragement for something you did or created, which meant a great deal to you? This is not about accolades or achievements; instead, it's an attempt to have you remember your earliest stirrings, which may still be within you today. Explore this topic now. You can also draw a representation of the item so that you will keep it at the top of your mind moving forward.

"Find something you're passionate
about and keep tremendously
interested in it."

— JULIA CHILD

UNDERSTAND THAT YOU SHOWED UP HERE AS A TINY INFANT CAPABLE OF AN INFINITE NUMBER OF POTENTIALITIES.

Many of your choices remain unexplored because of a hopefully well-intentioned conditioning program designed to make you fit the culture of your caretakers. You probably had next to no opportunity to disagree with the cultural and societal arrangements made for your life.

There may have been some adults who encouraged you to have an open mind, but if you're honest with yourself, you know that your philosophy of life, your religious beliefs, your manner of dress, and your language are a function of what others determined was right for you. If you made any fuss about going against this preordained conditioning, you probably heard even stronger voices insisting that you get back in line and do things the way they have "always been done." Fitting in superseded having a mind that was open to new ideas.

List any of the messages you've received over the years that discouraged you from pursuing your interests or being creative (or even curious). See how your mind completes the following prompts:

I cannot be _____ *until I . . .*

_____

_____

_____

_____

_____

If I ever _____ ,

I would disappoint those who depend on me.

_____

_____

_____

_____

_____

_____

_____

A successful life must contain . . .

_____

_____

_____

_____

_____

_____

_____

_____

_____

_____

WHAT YOU THINK ABOUT EXPANDS.

If you've gone through life with a closed mind, you have of necessity acted upon those closed-mind notions, and you'll see evidence of your thinking virtually everywhere you go.

What are some instances of this type of thinking in your past? Has a closed mind or some judgmental ideas impacted you or held you back from the life of your dreams? In what way?

On the other hand, should you decide (make no mistake about this, it is a choice) to have a mind that's open to everything, then you'll act upon that inner energy, and you'll be the creator as well as the recipient of miracles wherever you are.

What would it mean to start having an open mind; that is, to turn your back on old conditioning and see the world with fresh eyes? Look back at the negative beliefs you outlined in the previous exercise and consider what different choices you might have made had you never internalized those messages. How would it feel to know you could pursue the callings of your soul?

"A closed mind is a dying mind."

— EDNA FERBER

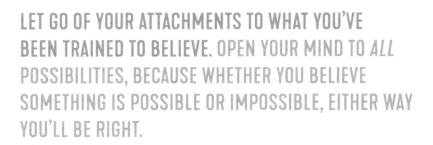

LET GO OF YOUR ATTACHMENTS TO WHAT YOU'VE BEEN TRAINED TO BELIEVE. OPEN YOUR MIND TO *ALL* POSSIBILITIES, BECAUSE WHETHER YOU BELIEVE SOMETHING IS POSSIBLE OR IMPOSSIBLE, EITHER WAY YOU'LL BE RIGHT.

Your agreement with reality and all that's possible determines what you'll become. So if you're convinced that you can't become wealthy, famous, artistic, a professional athlete, a great singer, or whatever, you will act upon that inner conviction that prevents you from manifesting what you'd really like. All that you'll get from your effort is being right.

What are some things that you have believed you couldn't become? How do you know these beliefs are "true"?

An open mind allows you to explore and create and grow. A closed mind seals off any such creative explanation. Remember that progress would be impossible if we did things the way we always have. So be sure to open yourself up to new ideas, especially if they come from those outside of your normal social circle. It's important to listen without judgment to what others have to say.

The ability to participate in miracles—true miracles in your life— happens when you open your mind to your limitless potential. Explore this topic here: What are some beliefs that you have dismissed as not possible or worth examining? Do you think you can open yourself up to new people and ideas now?

You always have a choice in how you react to anything that life offers you.

AS YOU ARE ENGAGING WITH OTHER PEOPLE, IT IS IMPORTANT THAT YOU ARE ALWAYS, *ALWAYS* TRUE TO YOURSELF. YOU CAN ABSOLUTELY BE RESEPECTFUL OF OTHERS WHILE STILL CHOOSING TO DO WHAT IS RIGHT FOR YOU.

You have a choice: Will you take the unfamiliar and perhaps risky path? Or will you choose to not examine your beliefs and stay with the version of your life implanted in you by familial and cultural influences dictating precisely who you are and what your aspirations ought to be?

So many people don't believe they have choices; they feel that their problems have been imposed upon them by external factors over which they have zero control. When I was a therapist in private practice, I repeatedly offered my clients tools that would facilitate their discovering that they are the sum total of all of the choices they make. They'd always resist at first, wanting to blame or make excuses, and I'd point out *that* was a choice.

It can be scary to let go of all those beliefs about your limitations. You then have absolutely no one to blame when things don't go the way you wanted them to go. It is necessary, however, to take total responsibility for every single aspect of the journey you are undertaking.

Make a pledge to yourself now. Say: "I am committed to following my bliss. The Universe cooperates with me in bringing this to fruition. The right people will show up, the obstacles will be swept away, the necessary circumstances will materialize, and guidance will be there."

TAKING RESPONSIBILITY FOR YOUR LIFE AND CHOICES IS VERY EMPOWERING.

When you do, it's as if you're saying, "I may not understand *why* I feel this way, why I have this illness, why I've been victimized, or why I had this accident, but I'm willing to say without any guilt or resentment that I own it. I live with, and I am responsible for, having it in my life."

Why do this? If you take responsibility for having it, then at least you have a chance to also take responsibility for removing it or learning from it. If you're in some small (perhaps unknown) way responsible for that physical pain or that emotional disturbance, then you can go to work to remove it or discover what its message is for you. If, on the other hand, someone or something else is responsible in your mind, then of course you'll have to wait until they change for you to get better. And that is unlikely to occur.

Reflect on a situation when you experienced something unwelcome. What did you have to gain from any apparent obstacles? Can you see what role you played in the circumstances and what you were responsible for attracting? (Later, we'll discuss how to use our minds to eliminate those unwelcome energies and shift our vibrations to those more harmonious with our purpose.)

THE GREATEST GIFT THAT ANY OF US ARE GRANTED IS THE GIFT OF OUR IMAGINATION.

Every single thing that now exists was once imagined . . . everything that is ever going to exist in the future must first be imagined. Yet I have so often noticed that most people do not have even an inkling of the power that exists within them if they learn to apply the extraordinary capacity of their own minds.

If you want to accomplish anything, you must first be able to expect it of yourself. If you can't imagine it, you can't create it. So let's try using your imagination now. Write down what your ideal life would be like—for example, what would each day entail? Take some time to close your eyes and engage all your senses: What would you like to see, hear, smell, taste, and touch? The idea is to get as detailed as possible, to start flexing the awesome power of your imagination.

"What the imagination seizes as Beauty must be truth—whether it existed before or not."

— JOHN KEATS

SUPPOSE YOU HAD A CHOICE BETWEEN TWO MAGIC WANDS. WITH WAND A, YOU CAN HAVE ANY PHYSICAL THING YOU DESIRE BY SIMPLY WAVING IT. WITH WAND B, YOU CAN HAVE A SENSE OF PEACE FOR THE REST OF YOUR LIFE REGARDLESS OF WHAT CIRCUMSTANCES ARISE.

Which would you pick? A guarantee of stuff or inner peace for the remainder of your life? If you opt for peace, then you already have Wand B.

It's important to understand that if you are focused on acquiring things, that isn't a purpose. Enjoy it all, sure, but never make your happiness or success dependent on an attachment to any thing, any place, and, particularly, any person.

Returning to the last exercise, what undergirds your ideal life is how it *makes you feel*. If you wrote about quitting your job or winning the lottery, for instance, what's underneath all of that is most likely a desire for a life of freedom. So if you take another look at what you wrote with this new lens, what jumps out at you?

Listen to your heart, and express the music that you hear.

TAKE A MOMENT RIGHT NOW AND POINT TO YOURSELF. I'LL BET YOUR FINGER IS POINTING RIGHT AT YOUR HEART. NOT AT YOUR BRAIN, BUT YOUR HEART. THIS IS WHO YOU ARE.

Next, think of a situation and ask yourself if what you *know* or what you *feel* is most important to you. Generally, what you'll take care of first depends on the situation and circumstances you're in. Your logical brain can be figuring out exactly how you're supposed to act in a relationship when things are collapsing (or when they're rapturous), and then there are times when your intuitive heart will supersede what you know.

If you *are* feeling fearful, scared, lonely—or on the other hand, thrilled, loving, and ecstatic—these will be the dominant forces you'll act upon. These are the times when your intuition is right. Your heart will always lead you passionately to your purpose.

What does logic tell you is the purpose of life? Now tune in to your heart. What does it say is your purpose? Write or draw what you feel on these next two pages.

THE PURPOSE OF LIFE (ACCORDING TO LOGIC)

THE PURPOSE OF LIFE (ACCORDING TO MY HEART)

WE ALL HAVE A DESTINY, A DHARMA TO FULFILL, AND THERE ARE ENDLESS OPPORTUNITIES, PEOPLE, AND CIRCUMSTANCES THAT SURFACE THROUGHOUT OUR LIVES TO ILLUMINATE OUR PATH.

These create tiny sparks that cause us to recognize, *This is for me—this is important; this is why I'm here.* Those sparks are signals to pay attention and be astonished and know that they are being ignited by the same Divine Source that is responsible for all of creation.

I have always been eager to say yes to life in the belief that when I trust in myself, I am trusting in the very wisdom that created me. That inner spark is God talking to me, and I simply refuse to ignore it. I know that if I feel it and it ignites something in me, then the igniting process is the invisible, the Source, the very essence of all creation—and I trust it to the max.

Cultivating your own ability to recognize those sparks starts with paying attention to your intuition. The more you trust in your heart, the more you will see how all things are in pure alignment with your own dharma.

Have you already felt those sparks of recognition? Or can you think of other times when your heart pulled you so strongly toward something that you now know is part of your purpose?

WE LIVE IN A NOISY WORLD, CONSTANTLY BOMBARDED WITH LOUD MUSIC, SIRENS, CONSTRUCTION EQUIPMENT, JET AIRPLANES, RUMBLING TRUCKS, LEAF BLOWERS, LAWN MOWERS, AND TREE CUTTERS.

So many human-made, unnatural sounds invade our senses and keep silence at bay. In fact, we've been raised in a culture that not only eschews silence but is terrified of it. The car radio must always be on, and any pause in conversation is a moment of embarrassment that most people quickly fill with chatter. For many, being alone is a nightmare, and being alone in silence is pure torture.

How do you feel about sitting in silence? If someone gave you the gift of an hour of nothing to do, but you had to do it in silence, with no distractions, would you welcome it? Write down your thoughts on this here.

"When the whole
world is silent, even one
voice becomes powerful."

— MALALA YOUSAFZAI

I URGE YOU TO EMBRACE SILENCE, AND TO DEMAND MORE AND MORE TIME FOR IT IN YOUR LIFE.

One of the most effective ways to do this is to make meditation a daily practice. Explore the many different types out there to see what practice resonates with you. And remember, there's no such thing as a bad meditation.

I try to meditate each time I stop at a red light. With the car stopped and my body inactive, frequently the only things still moving are the thoughts in my mind. I use those two minutes or so at the stoplight to bring my mind into harmony with my inert car and body. I get a wonderful bonus of silence. I probably stop at a red light 20 or 30 times a day, creating 40 minutes to an hour of silence. And there's always someone behind me to let me know that my time is up by breaking the silence with a honking horn!

Try this: repeat the sound of *ahhhh* in the morning and *om* in the evening for approximately 20 minutes. This creates an opportunity for you to experience inner serenity, in a way you may have never known before. (If you would like to learn more about meditation, there are many wonderful books, audio programs, videos, and practitioners to help; you could also begin with my book *Getting in the Gap*.)

How can you start incorporating more silence and meditation into your life? Use this space to jot down notes about practices you're interested in or already doing. Plan a schedule, and try to stick to it. Even five minutes in the morning, or before you go to sleep, or as you begin or end your commute would be a great start. Come back to this page periodically, and write any results you notice here.

Anytime in your life when you're feeling out of sorts in any way, go to nature and find your peace.

NATURE HAS A MARVELOUS WAY OF HEALING MANY MALADIES.

If you ever suffer from insomnia, walk barefoot on the grass for 10 minutes before getting into bed. Blissful sleep is sure to follow.

Or try spending a day in an isolated spot, listening only to the sounds of nature—the birds, the insects, the rustling of leaves, the wind. These are the sounds of healing that can offset the painful sounds of 18-wheelers, cement mixers, loud stereos, and the like.

Give yourself opportunities to be in the wilderness as a regular part of your life routine. Jot down a few ideas now for places you can connect with nature. What can you do today? This week? This month? Think of places that you can go to spontaneously as well as aspirational places that might take some planning. Try to commit to at least one day each month to be alone and commune with nature—this is the ultimate therapy.

FIND AN OPPORTUNITY TO OBSERVE A LITTLE GREEN SPROUT EMERGING FROM A SEED.

Allow yourself to feel the awe of what you're seeing, even if you're just looking at time-lapse videos online. The scene of an emerging sprout represents the beginning of life, yet no one on this planet has even a tiny clue as to how all of this works. What is that creative spark that causes the life to sprout? What created the observer, the consciousness, the observation, and perception itself? The questions are endless.

As you are feeling that awe of creation, keep in mind that whatever universal law that has ever been utilized to manifest a miracle anywhere, anytime, and in anything (including that seed!) is still on the books. It has never been repealed, and it never will be. You posess the same energy to be a miracle worker—but only if you truly believe and know it within yourself.

Allow yourself to sit with the knowledge that you are a part of that creative, loving, miraculous energy. When you feel ready, express what this exercise brought up for you, either visually or in words.

YOU ARE A DIVINE CREATION, AND YOU CAN NEVER BE SEPARATE FROM THAT WHICH CREATED YOU.

If you can think of God as the ocean, and yourself as a container, you may find it helpful in moments of doubt or feeling lost or alone to remember that you are a container of God. When you dip your glass into the ocean, what you have is a glass of God. It's not as big or as strong, but it's still God. As long as you refuse to believe otherwise, you won't feel separate from God.

When you do feel separate from God, you lose your Divine power, the power of your Source, which is the unlimited power to create, to be miraculous, and to experience the joy of being alive. Your ego is what's responsible for this disconnect. That's why it is imperative for you to tame that ego and treasure your Divinity.

This may be an uncomfortable topic for some—how does it make you feel?

"You are a miracle,
and everything you touch
could be a miracle."

— THICH NHAT HANH

BEFORE WE SHOWED UP IN FORM, OUR MIND AND THE MIND OF GOD WERE SYNONYMOUS, WHICH MEANS THAT WE WERE FREE FROM THE BONDS OF THE EGO MIND.

When we're in harmony with our Divine nature, we simply don't have thoughts that tell us we can't accomplish something—our thoughts are of a higher energy.

Your ego wants you to live in a state of self-importance, but the only thing that's truly important is being in alignment with Spirit. You must work every day to tame ego's demands. If you're not sure how to do this, start by examining a few of the beliefs you have about who you are and what you deserve. Do these feel driven by external, ego-dominated energy, such as "I deserve to be rich and famous"? Write about that below.

Focusing on Spirit can help with taming the ego. For example, try repeating this affirmation: *My life is bigger than I am*. Write it out and strategically post it where you will see it regularly, such as in your home, car, or workplace. Remember that the "I" is your ego identification. Your life is Spirit flowing through you unhindered by ego—it's what you showed up here to actualize—and is infinite. The "I" that identifies you is a fleeting snippet.

Write below about how it feels when you tune in to Spirit and tune out the ego.

YOU ALWAYS HAVE THE POWER TO BRING YOURSELF INTO HARMONY WITH WHO YOU REALLY ARE: DIVINE ENERGY IN PHYSICAL FORM.

Spirit is a creating, giving, abundant, loving, joyful, nonjudgmental, all-things-are-possible, invisible mechanism. It is always giving, always serving, always in endless supply. Your job is to align with this frequency while simultaneously disabling your old, ego-dominated thought frequencies. Being stuck in lack, busyness, lost opportunities, bad luck, and so on is a misalignment with the frequencies of your original nature.

Practice catching yourself when you're engaged in the habit of negative thinking. Write about what happens as you're learning to monitor any thought that expresses, *It can't, It won't,* or *It's not my luck* and change it to an aligned thought such as, *It will, It must,* or *It's already here and I know it will arrive on schedule with Divine timing.* Do you find that this becomes easier the more you try it?

THERE IS A FAMOUS QUOTATION FROM THE CZECH WRITER AND POET FRANZ KAFKA, WHICH IS ONE OF MY FAVORITES: "YOU NEED NOT DO ANYTHING. REMAIN SITTING AT YOUR TABLE AND LISTEN. YOU NEED NOT EVEN LISTEN, JUST WAIT. YOU NEED NOT EVEN WAIT, JUST LEARN TO BE QUIET, STILL, AND SOLITARY. AND THE WORLD WILL FREELY OFFER ITSELF TO YOU UNMASKED. IT HAS NO CHOICE, IT WILL ROLL IN ECSTASY AT YOUR FEET."

This quote not only inspired me to write about and explore meditation, it also prompted my wife and me to raise our children in an atmosphere where silence and listening were emphasized over clamor and pandemonium.

You've probably had times in your life in which you needed to make a decision and did not know what to do. You may have felt afraid of doing the wrong thing or letting others down. Understand that every thought you have in which you're in a state of fear keeps you away from your purpose, and is simultaneously weakening you. Your fearful thoughts are inviting you to stay immobilized.

From this point on, when you find yourself afraid to make a decision, stop right there and invite God onto the scene. Turn fear over to your Senior Partner with these words: "I don't know how to deal with this, but I know I'm connected to You, the miraculous creative force in this Universe. I'll move my ego out of the way and turn it over to You." And then do what you say—step out of the way and let the answer come. You'll be surprised by how quickly that higher energy of love will nullify and dissolve your fearful thoughts and empower you at the same time.

"Never be afraid to sit
awhile and think."

— LORRAINE HANSBERRY

IN A UNIVERSE THAT'S AN INTELLIGENT SYSTEM WITH A DIVINE CREATIVE FORCE SUPPORTING IT, THERE SIMPLY CAN BE NO ACCIDENTS.

As tough as it is to acknowledge, you have had to go through whatever you've gone through in order to get to where you are today, and the evidence is that you did. Every spiritual advance that you will make in your life will very likely be preceded by some kind of fall or seeming disaster. Those dark times, accidents, tough episodes, periods of impoverishment, illnesses, abuses, and broken dreams were all in order. They happened, so you can assume they *had* to and you can't *un*happen them.

Embrace the tough times in your personal history from that perspective, with help from a therapist or friend if you need it. Understand them, accept them, and honor them. With the awareness that there is some sort of meaning associated with everything that arrives in your life, you can start to view all these events—in particular, those that result in dramatic shifts—as guidance from this Divine organizing intelligence that will not allow "accidents" to occur. This breaks the hold that these memories have on you.

It can also be helpful to come up with a ceremony to transform the energy of the past in your own way. For example, you could write a letter to the incident, describing everything that happened to you because of it, and then burn it (safely, of course). This would serve to release your attachment to it, making room for you to move forward in freedom.

Write about how you were able to embrace the lessons of the past, either with the help of another person or through a ceremony you came up with. What happened after you did this, and how are you feeling now?

Embrace
everything that
has happened
to you, and
move on to the
next act.

YOUR PAST IS OVER!

Become free to immerse yourself in this moment, the now that is the present. It's called that because it is in fact a present to open, relish, nurture, play with, and enjoy and explore.

It's doubtful that other creatures on earth waste the present in thoughts of past and future. A beaver only does beaver, and he does it right in the moment. He doesn't spend his days wishing he were a young beaver again. He's always in the now. We can learn much from such creatures about enjoying the present moment rather than using it up consumed with guilt over the past or worry about the future.

If you were to describe your present, would you call it a gift? Why or why not? What would it mean to let go of your past, and move on unencumbered?

IN RELEASING YOUR PAST, YOU MUST ALSO MAKE A PARTICULAR EFFORT TO REMOVE ALL LABELS THAT YOU'VE PLACED ON YOURSELF.

You're not an American, an Italian, or an African, for instance. You're a member of one race, the human race. You're not your sex or your gender, your job or your political party. You are one with the true oneness.

Labels serve to negate you. They make it so that you must ultimately live up to the label rather than being the limitless, Divine energy that is your true essence. Transcending them, particularly the ones that have been placed on you by others in your past, opens you to the opportunity of soaring in the now in any way that you desire. You can be all things at any present moment in your life.

Spend a few minutes writing down all the labels you've been given.

NOW REPLACE ALL THOSE LABELS WITH A KNOWING THAT YOU'RE NOT WHAT YOU'VE DONE, WHAT YOU'VE BEEN, HOW OTHERS HAVE TAUGHT YOU, OR WHAT HAS BEEN DONE TO YOU. **YOU'RE A PART OF THE BELOVED, CONNECTED ALWAYS TO SPIRIT, AND THEREFORE CONNECTED TO THE UNLIMITED POWER OF THE BELOVED.**

AS YOU LEARN TO LET GO OF LABELS, THERE'S ONE IN PARTICULAR THAT I WANT TO BRING YOUR ATTENTION TO NOW: FAILURE.

Maybe when you think of the past, you feel you've failed in some way. Well, there is no failure, only feedback—everything that you do produces a result. As I often told my children, "True nobility is not about being better than someone else, it's about being better than you used to be." In other words, rather than labeling yourself as a failure and then having to live with that label, see yourself as someone who learns from their experiences so that the results are much better next time.

Also, keep in mind that failure is a judgment. It's just an opinion. It's another label that comes from your fears, which can be eliminated by love. Love for yourself. Love for what you do. Love for others. Love for your planet. When you have love within you, fear cannot survive. There is such wisdom in this ancient saying: "Fear knocked at the door. Love answered and no one was there."

Think of a situation that you labeled as a "failure." How can you retell the story from the perspective of love?

"I really think a champion is
defined not by their wins,
but by how they can recover
when they fall."

— SERENA WILLIAMS

FOR MANY PEOPLE, IF THEY HAVE MORE THAN OTHERS, THEY FEEL BETTER ABOUT THEMSELVES. HAVING MORE MONEY MAKES THEM FEEL BETTER. ACCUMULATING MORE AWARDS AND PRESTIGE AND CLIMBING HIGHER ON THE CORPORATE LADDER ENCOURAGES THEM TO FEEL GOOD ABOUT THEMSELVES.

Ego consciousness prods you to compete, compare, and conclude that you are the best, so you concentrate on running faster and looking better than others. It's at this ego level of consciousness that problems exist. This is where inner peace is virtually impossible and success eludes you, because you must always be striving to be someplace else.

Feelings of despair, anger, hatred, bitterness, stress, and depression stem from the ego's anxiety and insistence on living up to an external standard. The result is the anguish of not measuring up or fitting in properly. The ego will seldom allow you to rest and demands more and more because it's terrified that you'll be called a failure. As I mentioned before, you must learn to tame this ever-demanding, impossible-to-satisfy ego. When you move beyond it and make your higher self the dominant force in your life, you'll begin to feel that contentment and inner glow of living your purpose.

Have the callings of your soul ever been interrupted by your ego? How did that feel at the time, and what do you think about it now? What might happen if you were to ignore it and listen to your higher self instead?

YOU HEAR PEOPLE SAY THIS ALL THE TIME: "I HAVE A RIGHT TO BE UPSET BECAUSE OF THE WAY I'VE BEEN TREATED. I HAVE A RIGHT TO BE ANGRY, HURT, DEPRESSED, SAD, AND RESENTFUL."

Learning to avoid this kind of thinking is one of my top secrets for living a life of purpose and happiness. Any time you're filled with resentment, you're turning the controls of your emotional life over to others to manipulate.

Many years ago, I saw this quote, which really resonated with me: "Resentment is letting someone you despise live rent-free inside your head." This is the problem with justifying any and all resentments. It takes away your peace and turns the controls of your inner world over to others, and often those others are people you dislike and want to stay as far removed from as possible.

Can you think of a time in your life in which resentment kept you from your purpose? How do you feel about it now—was that a good use of your time and energy?

"You may not control
all the events that happen
to you, but you can decide
not to be reduced by them."

— MAYA ANGELOU

THE REGULAR PRACTICE OF MEDITATION CAN ASSIST YOU IN AVOIDING ENERGIES SUCH AS RESENTMENT.

When you meditate, you radiate a different energy, making it easier for you to deflect the negativity of those you encounter. It is like having an invisible shield that nothing can penetrate. A hostile current is greeted with a smile and an inner knowing that this is not your "stuff." A person who attempts to bring you into their misery cannot succeed without your agreement.

Not only does your practice keep you immune to all that, but also it helps bring others into harmony with you. Studies confirm that meditation increases levels of serotonin (a neurotransmitter in your brain that indicates how peaceful and harmonious you feel) in practitioners. Amazingly, studies have also found that simply being in the vicinity of a large group of meditators raises the serotonin levels of the *observers*. In other words, the more you achieve peacefulness through meditation, the more your peaceful state impacts those around you.

Personally, after a meditation session, I find it almost impossible to be annoyed or negatively impacted by anything. It seems to bring me into contact with a current of soothing energy that makes me feel deeply connected to God.

Reflect on the situations you described in the previous exercise, when resentment held you back from your purpose. If you were to encounter similar circumstances in the future, how might you act differently with an increased sense of inner peace and a "shield" against negativity?

JUST AS NO ONE CAN DEFINE YOU WITH THEIR JUDGMENTS, NEITHER DO YOU HAVE THE PRIVILEGE OF JUDGING OTHERS.

Stop expecting those who are different to be what you think they should be. It's never going to happen. When you release your expectations and stop labeling others, and simply become an observer, you will know inner peace.

It's your ego that demands that the world and all the people in it be as you think they should be. Your higher, sacred self refuses to be anything but peaceful, and sees the world as it is, not as your ego would like it to be.

You can never get behind another person's eyeballs, so you have no idea what is going on in their life. Can you think of a time when you made an assumption about someone else that turned out to be wrong? How did you feel when you found out the truth?

"The essence of greatness
is the ability to choose
personal fulfillment in
circumstances where others
choose madness."

— VIKTOR FRANKL

There can be
no sides on a
round planet.

I WANT TO TELL YOU THAT WHATEVER YOU HAVE GOING ON IN THE WAY OF ANIMOSITY, BITTERNESS, ANGUISH, OR PAIN TOWARD ANY OTHER HUMAN BEING ON OUR PLANET, WHOEVER THEY ARE AND WHAT THEY'VE DONE—IF YOUR REACTION IS ONE OF TOXIC BITTERNESS, IT WILL NEVER LET GO OF YOU.

Forgiveness is the greatest motivator in the world. If you are hanging on to anything painful or hurtful toward anyone or anything, you've got to let go of it all.

The boundaries between yourself and other people start to break down when you realize that we're all one, and we all live on this one planet. But you've got to get back far enough to see the oneness that we come from, the oneness that we are, the oneness that all humanity is—that we are like one cell in this whole body called humanity.

Can you do this—can you stop noticing the things that supposedly separate you from other people? What if your boundaries become diffused, and you view each human being you meet not in terms of what separates you from them, but of what connects you to them? Rather than clinging to your separateness, try to reach toward others. See everyone out there as connected to you in some way, which gives you the freedom to build bridges instead of walls.

Take some time to think about all of this, and then express your feelings on the next two pages.

"We're all under the same sky and walk the same earth; we're alive together during the same moment."

— MAXINE HONG KINGSTON

LEARN TO BE VERY GOOD AT FORGIVING, AS IT IS ONE OF THE THE MOST HEALING THINGS THAT YOU CAN DO TO REMOVE THE NEGATIVE ENERGIES FROM YOUR LIFE.

You practice forgiveness for two reasons. One is to let others know that you no longer wish to be in a state of hostility with them; and two, to free yourself from the self-defeating energy of resentment. Resentment is like venom that continues to pour through your system, doing its poisonous damage long after being bitten by the snake. It's not the bite that kills you; it's the venom. You can remove venom by making a decision to let go of resentments. Send love in some form to those you feel have wronged you and notice how much better you feel, how much more peace you have.

The same thing applies to yourself: In fact, the importance of forgiving yourself cannot be stated strongly enough. If you carry around thoughts of shame about what you've done in the past, you're weakening yourself both physically and emotionally. Similarly, if you use a technique of shame and humiliation on anyone to get *them* to reform, you're going to create a weakened person who will never become empowered until those shameful and humiliating thoughts are removed. Removing your own thoughts of shame involves a willingness to let go, to see your past behaviors as lessons you had to learn, and to reconnect to your Source through prayer and meditation.

Bring to mind a particular situation in which you still hold judgment against another person or yourself. What would it take for you to forgive others—and, more importantly, yourself? Express your thoughts here.

HOW DO YOU WANT TO BE PERCEIVED IN THIS WORLD?

Anyone who responds that they don't care at all is either not being truthful or trying to live with blinders on. Of course you care! In some cases, your very livelihood depends on your response to this question. You want to enjoy relating in a joyful, playful, intimate, loving, helpful, concerned, caring, and thoughtful manner with others. It's the nature of all of our human relationships to want to give and receive those emotions, and to feel connected to one another.

The answer to how you want to be perceived in the world is, at its simplest: *I want to be seen as a truthful person.* You want the truth of who you believe you are to mesh with what you're projecting outward. To do this, you need to make a decision to realign yourself on an energetic basis to get the scales balanced between your idealized self and your realized self, as perceived by the majority of people in your life.

Do you feel that your words and actions are matching the truth of your inner thoughts? If they are in alignment, that's great! If there's a disconnect, however, how might you bring all of this together in harmony?

"The way to right wrongs
is to turn the light of
truth upon them."

— IDA B. WELLS

THE UNIVERSE IS A **VAST MIRROR REFLECTING BACK** TO YOU EXACTLY WHAT YOU ARE.

Are you projecting happy energy, or are you regularly told to "lighten up" or "chill out" and "stop letting yourself get so worked up"? If you're spending a great deal of time and energy finding opportunities to get upset, you will find them, whether it's a rude stranger, a fashion misstep, someone cursing, a sneeze, a black cloud, any cloud, an absence of clouds—just about anything will do.

Let joy be your habitual way of responding to the world rather than outrage. Here are some suggestions for adopting this perspective:

- Make a commitment to look for joy everywhere.

- Offer joyful commentary wherever possible.

- Reach out to others in cheerfulness.

- Go on an appreciation spree, rather than discussing the evils of the world.

- Use every opportunity to live joy, extend joy, radiate joy.

Come up with a few ideas of your own here. How can you radiate joy this week? Today? Right now?

Would you
rather be right
than kind?

MOST PEOPLE OPERATE FROM THE EGO AND REALLY NEED TO BE RIGHT.

So, when you encounter someone saying things that you find inappropriate, try to depersonalize what you just heard and respond with kindness.

Or when you know someone is wrong, wrong, wrong, forget your need to be right and instead say, "You're right about that!" Those words will end potential conflict and free you from feeling offended or judgmental. Remember, your desire is to be peaceful—not to be right, hurt, angry, or resentful. If you have enough faith in your own beliefs, you'll find that it's impossible to be offended by the beliefs and conduct of others.

Try this experiment, and write about the results below.

I'D LIKE TO RETURN TO THE IMPORTANCE OF STAYING IN THE PRESENT. OR, IN THE FAMOUS WORDS OF MY DEAR FRIEND RAM DASS, *BE HERE NOW.*

The willingness and ability to live fully in the now eludes many people. Try shifting your behavior so that while you're eating your appetizer, you're not concerned with dessert. While reading a book, notice where your thoughts are. While on vacation, be there instead of thinking about what should have been done and what has to be done when returning home. Don't let the elusive present moment get used up by thoughts that aren't in the here-and-now.

There's an irony to this habit of having your mind drift to other times and other places. You can only drift off in the now, because now is all you ever get. So drifting off is a way of using up your present moments. You do indeed have a past, but not now! And yes, you have a future, but not now! And you can consume your now with thoughts of "then" and "maybe," but that will keep you from the inner peace and success you could be experiencing right this second..

Does this ring true for you? Have you tended to be so consumed by the past or worried about the future that you can't fully be here now? If so, how might you shift your behavior moving forward?

"Remember then: there is
only one time that is important—
Now! It is the most important
time because it is the only time
when we have any power."

— LEO TOLSTOY

OUR RELATIONSHIP TO THE PRESENT MOMENT DEFINES OUR RELATIONSHIP TO LIFE ITSELF.

Consider these suggestions for implementing present-moment awareness:

- Practice becoming aware of your reactions when someone introduces any kind of mental disturbance into your life. Where do your thoughts take you? What do you think about in that instant? You'll probably find that your thoughts are projections into the past or the future, so bring yourself back to the now. As you're receiving the disrupting information, ask, *How am I feeling right now?* instead of *How am I going to feel later?* or *How did I feel back then?* By giving yourself a gentle reminder in the moment of your discomfort, you'll bring yourself back to what you're experiencing now. Watch as your discomfort dissolves when you return to the present. Keep practicing bringing yourself back to the here-and-now, and remember as you do so that this is your relationship to life. Accept the present moment and find the perfection that's untouched by time itself.

- Make meditation and yoga a daily part of your life. Begin today, practicing any form that appeals to you. You'll discover that you become adept at allowing thoughts to flow through in the now. It will help you be present and experience the oneness of everything.

- Repeat this affirmation: *I choose to stay fully present in the now.* By repeating this to yourself in silence for a five-minute period, you reinforce the importance of being a present-moment person. Repetition is crucial! Make this a regular practice and it will ultimately become your way of being.

Stay present: every second, every minute, and every hour. Every day of your life is full of present moments of infinite value. This is how you will stay tuned in to your purpose—and your Source.

WHEN YOU FEEL OUT OF SORTS, ASK YOURSELF: *DO I WISH TO USE THE PRESENT MOMENT—THE PRECIOUS CURRENCY OF MY LIFE—IN THIS MANNER?*

This will help you to become conscious of the importance of being here now—not just in your body, but in your thinking as well. I urge you to think of the present as just that: a wondrous present from your Source. Anytime you're filling the now with thoughts about how you used to be, concerns about what someone has done to harm you, or worries about the future, you're saying "No, thank you" to your Source for this precious gift.

Become conscious of just how valuable this present is. "This is the only moment you have," is a sentence I often say to myself to keep me on friendly terms with the now. Think about that: the only moment you have. When you realize the significance of this, you'll immediately want to shift into a state of awe and gratitude for it, regardless of what is transpiring.

I do this frequently in my yoga practice, particularly when I'm challenged by a difficult posture. Balancing on one leg and holding the other one straight out with my hands cupped beneath the ball of my foot is a challenge that leads me to murmur, "Be here now, Wayne. Just stay in the present moment."

Affirmations can be very helpful for this. Try: *I refuse to use my precious present moments in any way that takes me away from the Divine love from which I originated.* Or write your own here, along with any other thoughts you have on how you can use your present moments more optimally.

"All you need is deep within you waiting to unfold and reveal itself. All you have to do is be still and take time to seek for what is within, and you will surely find it."

— EILEEN CADDY

ON MANY MORNINGS I WOULD ENTER MY CHILDREN'S BEDROOMS AND PROVIDE THEIR WAKE-UP MESSAGE, SINGING IN A BOOMING VOICE, "OH, WHAT A BEAUTIFUL MORNING! GOSH, WHAT A BEAUTIFUL DAY!"

I would go on to tell them, "This is the only day of your life. There is no past, there is no future, there is only now—so go out and fully enjoy this day."

The kids would all grumble about their crazy father, but I truly wanted them to know and understand the message that Emily Dickinson offered with these five well-considered words, "Forever—is composed of Nows." Such a simple yet very profound idea, and one that I wanted my kids to grasp and live fully.

"You can't get out of now," I would regularly remind them. "Enjoy this day, this moment. Don't use a statement like, 'I'm not good at math,' or 'I'm clumsy,' or 'I'm not popular'—all based on something that happened in the past—as a reason for not excelling today in math, or not participating in a sporting event, or continuing to label yourself as shy or afraid. Instead, erase that personal history, and see your life today as a blank slate that you can fill in any way that you choose."

I love this proverb, which sums up beautifully the essence of this theme: "The best time to plant a tree is 20 years ago. The second best time is now." What this gets at is that you may feel as if you missed an opportunity, but you always have the option to begin. The time is now! So what have you been putting off? What do you know, deep in your heart, that it is now time to do?

WHEN YOU LIVE YOUR PURPOSE, YOU ARE GOING TO HAVE TO TAKE RISKS. THE PEOPLE IN YOUR LIFE MAY NOT UNDERSTAND WHAT YOU'RE DOING, BUT IF YOU BELIEVE IN YOURSELF, THAT NEEDS TO BE YOUR PRIORITY. YES, OTHERS MEAN WELL, BUT THEY CAN'T POSSIBLY KNOW WHAT'S RIGHT FOR YOU, AS THEY CAN'T HEAR WHAT CALLS TO YOUR SOUL.

I've taken a number of risks over the years, especially in terms of my career. I would like to take a moment here to tell you about what happened right after I wrote *Your Erroneous Zones* in 1976. The book was not exactly the bestseller it would become yet, and I was still a professor at St. John's University. I was driving on the Long Island Expressway when, without warning, clarity suddenly came over me. I pulled over onto the shoulder with tears running down my face, having the distinct feeling that I'd been enveloped by a loving guiding spirit. I knew what I *absolutely must do*.

I eased my way back onto the expressway, went to the university, and excitedly told the dean that I was resigning. I was told that this was a risky move in a very uncertain time and I would lose the benefits and job security that come with a professorship. But I had peered into my future and seen it as if it already were a present fact.

Alive with excitement, I cleaned out my desk, submitted my final grades, and headed off to my serenity spot a few blocks away. I spent the last 30 minutes of my career as a professor at St. John's University sitting atop a boulder, listening to the birds and the wind rustling through the branches. I was in a state of awe. I gave thanks for whatever it was that came over me, and gave me such luminous grace and clarity. I was for the very first time in my life, at the age of 36, self-employed, and I was flying by the seat of my pants, bewildered by the possibilities.

I did not know at the time that *Your Erroneous Zones* would be the first of dozens of books that I'd write over the next few decades, or that I was destined to impact the lives of millions of people all over the planet. I'm certain that the one Divine mind, the great Tao, God—or whatever we choose to call it—was fully aware of my purpose, and it must have known that I couldn't fulfill it from the comfort and safety of a professorship at a major university.

Something indefinable showed up for me that June day in 1976 and assisted me in making an uncomfortable shift in my life. It has happened on several occasions ever since, especially when I've been on the edge about what direction to take. I trust in these peak-experience moments and not only rely upon them, but invite them into my life. The more I've become confident in what my life's purpose is about, the more I've been able to access this kind of vivid, emotionally charged energy.

I include this story here because many folks seem to think that I just instantly became a best-selling author, when it actually took a lot of time and work. Most of all, it required me to listen to the callings of my soul and play the music I was meant to play, regardless of what other people thought or said.

THE SAME IS TRUE FOR YOU—YOUR HIGHER SELF IS GUIDING YOU TO LIVE YOUR OWN PURPOSE, AND YOU HAVE THE POWER TO TAKE WHATEVER RISKS YOU NEED TO. YOU CAN DO IT!

LET'S LOOK AT SOME OF THE EXCUSES THAT MIGHT BE HOLDING YOU BACK FROM LIVING YOUR PURPOSE.

If you are a parent, there may be a part of you that is resistant to putting yourself first. Well, there is a fundamental axiom that both my wife and I practiced in the raising of our children and it is this: *Parents are not for leaning upon, but rather exist to make leaning unnecessary*. We wanted to raise self-reliant children to become successful and peaceful adults, and that's exactly what happened.

Children respond positively when they see that their parents are happy and engaged in life. In fact, anyone who genuinely loves you is going to want the best for you. Worrying about what anyone else might think or say is just another barrier to your success and inner peace.

Are you inspired when you see others living their truth? How can you live your life as inspiration to others (children, loved ones, neighbors, mentees, acquaintances, and so on) to live their own dreams?

"The struggle has always been inner, and is played out in outer terrains. Awareness of our situation must come before inner changes, which in turn come before changes in society. Nothing happens in the 'real' world unless it first happens in the images in our heads."

— GLORIA ANZALDÚA

THE "IT'S TOO BIG" EXCUSE SEEMS TO PLOP ON TOP OF PEOPLE AND TOTALLY IMMOBILIZE THEM ON THE PATH TO LIVING THEIR PURPOSE.

Perhaps surprisingly, this belief only needs to be reversed. If you believe that people are successful because they think big, for instance, I'm here to tell you that success demands small thinking! Bring this realization into your consciousness and you will have accessed the ability to think small and begin tackling the big issue of fulfilling your purpose.

While you can't get humongous things done today, you can take that first step. While you can't receive your Ph.D. today, you can register for a course that begins next week, and that's all you can do regarding that lofty goal for now. Think small and accomplish what you can in the here-and-now.

This perspective can be applied to any large task. If you'd like to quit drinking alcohol or smoking cigarettes, you can't do so for the next ten years with a single action. But you can refuse to give in to your addictions today, or even smaller, in this moment. That you can do. And that is precisely how all habituated thinking habits get changed: by thinking and acting small in the now moment and living the only way that anyone really does live—one minute, one hour, one day at a time.

Select a goal of yours now. It can be one related to your purpose, but if that seems too "big" right now, just pick any goal. Brainstorm action steps you can accomplish within a minute, an hour, and a day at a time.

DO YOU FEAR THAT NO ONE WOULD HELP YOU FULFILL YOUR PURPOSE AND **YOU CAN'T GO IT ALONE?**

The fact is that the world is filled with people who would jump at the chance to help you with whatever you'd like to create. But if you hold on to a false notion that no one will be there to help you, your experiences will match that belief. Once that belief begins changing, you'll see help arriving, but the initial movement is completely in your thoughts. It begins with this new belief: *I can access help.*

I often repeat this thought from *A Course in Miracles*: "If you knew who walked beside you at all times on this path that you have chosen, you could never experience fear or doubt again." It helps me remember my purpose and that I am never alone.

I affirm that all that is needed or required will be there, and I consciously encourage myself with this unquestionable certainty. And help seems to come from all directions: The money I need somehow shows up, the right people emerge, and circumstances occur that are unexpectedly helpful—almost as if some synchronistic force steps in and bewilders me with the beauty of it all! I'm encouraged by my unquestionable power to elevate myself in any situation.

Begin encouraging yourself with affirmations that support and elevate your beliefs. These will help to align you with the channel of energy that's always available to your true Divine nature. Take inspiration from the following affirmations, and then come up with some of your own.

I have the capacity to create by myself if necessary.
I know the right people to help me are here at the right time.
The world is full of people who would love to assist me.

ACCEPTING THE BELIEF THAT YOU "DON'T HAVE THE ENERGY" TO FOLLOW YOUR BLISS IS PART OF A LEARNED RESPONSE.

The prospect of making significant changes in your life can be daunting, so you hang on to old and comfortable behavior patterns by using the excuse of tiredness.

You may be proud that you've discovered your life purpose: *I'm meant to be a healer!* You may have found the next small step to take: *I can learn the skills at this school for that career path!* But then when it comes time to enroll, something always comes up: *I've got too much going on at work right now, I won't have the energy to take care of my kids and go to school,* and so on. . . .

Low energy is by and large not a problem of body chemistry—it's a function of a long history of habituated thinking. You have the power to use your thoughts to elevate yourself to new levels of success, happiness, and health. You can learn to practice more satisfying and vibrant thinking that will raise your enthusiasm, and ultimately produce an energetic lifestyle filled with purpose.

In my own life, I noticed that the more I said the words *I'm tired,* the more my energy seemed to be depleted, even when there were no physical reasons behind this. One morning after listening to a friend tell me that he was too exhausted to carry out a planned weekend retreat, I decided to end my use of this excuse permanently. I pledged to never again tell others (or myself) how tired I was, and I began to imagine myself in possession of unlimited energy. I didn't change my lifestyle or my sleep habits—all I did was imagine myself as a high-energy person. I was able to change the way I viewed myself in relationship to fatigue and started to see myself as a never-tired person. This all started with a new thought, which was placed first in my imagination.

Refuse to cater to low-energy mental activity. Be determined to unquestionably place your thoughts not on what you *can't* do, but on what you *intend* to create. Stay in this mind-set and you'll never want to use the low-energy excuse again.

Can you see yourself as a high-energy person? Write a story, draw a picture, or come up with affirmations to support this new vision of you.

WHEN IT COMES TO WHY PEOPLE ARE NOT LIVING AT THE HIGHEST LEVELS, THE EXCUSE OF "I'M TOO BUSY" EASILY TOPS THE LIST. I'LL BET THIS SOUNDS FAMILIAR TO YOU AS WELL.

Yet again, this all comes down to choice—that is, if you're overextended, you have chosen to be in this position. All the activities of your life, including those that take up huge portions of your time, are simply the result of the decisions you've made. If your family responsibilities are problematic, you've opted to prioritize your life in this way. If your calendar is crammed, you've decided to live with a full schedule. If there are way too many small details that only you can handle, then this, again, is a choice you've made.

Surely, one of the major purposes of life is to be happy. If you're using the excuse that you're too busy to be happy, you've made a *choice* to be busy. If you've substituted being busy for actively and happily fulfilling your destiny, you need to reexamine your priorities.

Write down all the tasks and details that occupy your attention. What areas take up most of your time? Are these the same areas you feel are important for a life lived with purpose?

WORK TO CHANGE THIS PATTERN OF BUSYNESS BY NEVER SAYING OR IMPLYING THAT YOU'RE TOO BUSY. PRACTICE DELEGATING, GETTING OTHERS TO HELP OUT, AND TAKING TIME FOR YOURSELF.

Repeat the following affirmation: *I intend to take time for myself to live the life that I came here to live, and to do it without ignoring my responsibilities as a parent, spouse, or employee.*

What might your life look life if you were to make this change? You can write a story, draw a picture, or even come up with a daily schedule that reflects your new life.

"Every moment is an
organizing opportunity, every
person a potential activist,
every minute a chance to
change the world."

— DOLORES HUERTA

We become
what we think about
all day long—this is
one of the greatest
secrets that so many
people are unaware of
as they pursue their
life's purpose.

WHATEVER IT IS THAT YOU ENVISION FOR YOURSELF— NO MATTER HOW LOFTY OR IMPOSSIBLE IT MAY SEEM TO YOU RIGHT NOW—I ENCOURAGE YOU TO BEGIN *ACTING AS IF* WHAT YOU WOULD LIKE TO BECOME IS ALREADY YOUR REALITY.

This is a wonderful way to set into motion the forces that will collaborate with you to make your dreams come true. And know this for certain: Whatever it may be, you can make a living doing it and simultaneously provide a service for others. I guarantee it.

Write your vision for yourself here.

THE USE OF THE TWO MAGIC WORDS *I AM* IS A WONDERFUL TECHNIQUE FOR ALIGNING WITH ONE'S SOURCE OF BEING.

These are the words spoken to Moses when he asked for the name of the spirit who spoke to him in the form of a burning bush that was not being consumed.

There's a reason that affirmations are always phrased in the present, using "I am" instead of "I want." It's because the use of these two words to declare what you would like to materialize, such as *I am in perfect health* or *I am in a Divine relationship*—even if your senses tell you otherwise—is how your highest self operates on this earthly plane.

List some affirmations that apply to living your purpose here. I have included some to get you started here, but I highly recommend that you come up with your own. Then pick several that really speak to you, and place them on or near your vision board for extra manifesting power.

I am free to be myself.

I can accomplish anything I choose.

I am a worthy and valuable person.

I deserve health, happiness, and success.

I am guided by my desire to serve others rather than following the rules.

WHEN YOU SEE YOURSELF AS WHAT YOU'D LIKE TO BECOME, YOU TAKE CHARGE OF YOUR OWN DESTINY.

Right now, gather your courage to declare yourself as already being where you want to be. In so doing, you will almost force yourself to act in a new, exciting, and spiritual fashion. For example, if you're living a life of scarcity, and all the nice things that many people have are not coming your way, perhaps it's time to change your thinking and act *as if* what you enjoy having is already here.

Let's apply this principle to the area of your vocation. Place your thoughts on what it is you'd like to have or become—an artist, a musician, a computer programmer, a dentist, or whatever. In your thoughts, begin to picture yourself as having the skills to do these things. No doubts. Only a knowing. Then begin acting as if these things were already your reality. As an artist, for example, your vision allows you to draw, to visit art museums, to talk with famous artists, and to immerse yourself in the art world. In other words, you begin to *act* as an artist in all aspects of your life. In this way, you're getting out in front of yourself and taking charge of your own destiny at the same time that you're cultivating inspiration.

This week, start doing one concrete thing to help you act as if you are indeed living your purpose. Write down the results here.

If you can
see it, you
can be it.

WHAT ARE SOME IMAGES THAT REPRESENT THE LIFE YOU WANT TO LIVE?

Let's say it's symbolized by a new car: Find a photograph that matches your vision. Then take that picture and paste it on your bedroom door, as well as on the refrigerator. While you're at it, paste it on the dashboard of the car you're now driving! Visit a showroom, sit in "your" car, and note the beautiful new-car aroma. Run your hands over the seats, and grip the steering wheel. Walk all around your car, appreciating the lines of it. Take your car for a test drive, and visualize that you're entitled to drive this car, that you're inspired by its beauty, and that it's going to find a way into your life. In some way, somehow, this is your car.

You may be familiar with the concept of a vision board, as it's a very popular (and powerful) tool for manifesting. So, just like the example above, find images that represent your purpose, and paste them on a piece of poster board. Place the board someplace prominent, where you can look at it several times a day, and see yourself ultimately living the life of your dreams. Alternatively, draw or tape images, words, or quotes to the next few pages of this book.

MY LIFE OF PURPOSE

MY LIFE OF PURPOSE

AS YOU PLACE MORE AND MORE OF YOUR ENERGY ON WHAT YOU INTEND TO MANIFEST, YOU'LL START SEEING THOSE INTENTIONS MATERIALIZING.

It's best not to divulge your private insights to others, though. When you do so, you may often feel the need to explain and defend your ideas. Once the ego is present, the manifesting stops.

Go back to the description of your ideal life that you wrote at the beginning of this journal. Now spend some time acting as if you are wealthy, confident, free, or what have you. Note how your life starts to match what you've written below.

"You can't just sit there and wait for people to give you that golden dream. You've got to get out there and make it happen for yourself."

— DIANA ROSS

TREAT EVERYONE YOU ENCOUNTER WITH THE SAME INTENTION.

Celebrate in others their finest qualities. Treat them all in this "as if" manner, and I guarantee you that they will respond accordingly to your highest expectations. It's all up to you. Whether you think this is possible or impossible, either way you'll be right. And you'll see the rightness of your thoughts manifesting everywhere you go.

When you act toward your children, parents, siblings, and even more distant relatives as if the relationship was great and going to stay that way, and you point out their greatness rather than their goofiness, it is their greatness that you will see. In your relationship to your significant other, be sure to apply this principle as frequently as you can. If things aren't going well, ask yourself, "Am I treating this relationship as it is, or as I would like it to be?" So how do you want it to be? Peaceful? Harmonious? Mutually satisfying? Respectful? Loving? Of course you do. So before your next encounter, see it in those ways. Have expectations that focus on the qualities of inner peace and success.

You'll find yourself pointing out what you love about that person rather than what they're doing wrong. You'll also see that other person responding back to you in love and harmony rather than in an embittered way. Your ability to get out in front of yourself and see the outcome before it transpires will cause you to act in ways that bring about these results.

Write down what happens here.

Attitude is everything, so pick a good one.

ON THE EXIT DOOR TO MY WRITING SPACE AT MY OFFICE, I PLACED THAT SIMPLE WRITTEN OBSERVATION YOU SEE ON THE PREVIOUS PAGE.

This was my daily reminder to be cognizant of my thoughts, and to persistently remember that any and all negative or fearful thoughts could and would impact everything I experienced each day—most especially, my own physical health.

I invite you to copy these words, and place them where you can see them as well. If other observations or lines catch your attention, write them down here.

THE MIND IS A POWERFUL TOOL IN CREATING HEALTH, DIVINE RELATIONSHIPS, ABUNDANCE, HARMONY IN BUSINESS—AND EVEN PARKING PLACES!

If your thoughts are focused on what you want to attract in your life, and you maintain that thought with the passion of an absolute intention, you'll eventually act upon that intention, because the ancestor to every single action is a thought.

Be aware at any given moment in your life that you always have a choice about the thoughts you allow in your mind. No one else can put a thought there. Regardless of the circumstances you find yourself in, it is your choice. Choose to replace disempowering, weakening thoughts with thoughts of a higher spiritual frequency.

Don't convince yourself that it can't be done or it's easier said than done. Your mind is yours to control. You are the creator and selector of your thoughts. You can change them at will. It is your God-given inheritance, your corner of freedom that no one can take away. No one can have control of your thoughts without your consent. So choose to avoid thoughts that weaken you, and you will know true wisdom. It is your choice!

Write down what you are learning about the power of your mind here.

THERE SIMPLY ARE **NO LIMITS.**

When you place something into your imagination, and hold on to that inner vision as if it were affixed with superglue, that is how you align with your Source of being. It is a way of being a co-creator with God, Who is responsible for all of creation. This is how you connect with your Senior Partner, and this is how the whole process of manifestation unfolds.

I have written extensively about this power of manifestation, and have often said, "If you place your thoughts on what you don't want, don't be at all surprised if what you don't want keeps showing up in your life."

Similarly, I encourage you to avoid placing your thoughts on what others expect of you, or on what has always been, or on what is difficult or impossible, unless that is what you want to manifest into your life.

Repeat the following mantra to yourself for a minimum of five straight minutes each day: *I am surrounded by the conditions I wish to attract into my life.* Say it quickly and repeatedly, even if it sounds ludicrous to do so. The repetition will help you begin to imagine the right people or circumstances, the necessary funding, or whatever it is you desire. Stay detached and allow the Universe to take care of the details. Then write down any changes you notice.

"Don't be limited by others'
limited imaginations."

— MAE JEMISON

The purpose of life is to
live a life of purpose.

I'VE LEARNED THROUGH THE YEARS THAT THE INNER MANTRA OF THE EGO IS ALWAYS SOME VARIATION OF, *WHAT'S IN IT FOR ME? TAKE CARE OF ME—I'M THE MOST IMPORTANT PERSON IN THE WORLD.*

As much as personal goals are important, it's far more important to tame the demands of the ego. Practice giving and serving without expectation of reward (or even a thank-you)—and let your reward be spiritual fulfillment.

To access Divine guidance in making your life work at the highest levels of happiness, success, and health, you must take the focus off of *Gimme, gimme, gimme.* Instead, place it on *How may I serve? What may I offer? How can I help?* When you do, the Universe will respond similarly, asking, *How may I serve you? What may I offer you? How can I help you?*

How can you practice higher awareness by serving others and the world?

"Every single one of us matters, has a role to play, makes a difference. We cannot live through a day without impacting the world around us—and we have a choice: what sort of impact do we want to make?"

— JANE GOODALL

YOU WILL DEFINITELY FIND YOURSELF FEELING PURPOSEFUL IF YOU CAN FIND A WAY TO BE IN THE SERVICE OF OTHERS.

Purpose is about serving. You build because you love to build—but you also build to make others happy. You design because your heart directs you to—and also those designs are in the service of others. You write because you love to express yourself in words—but also those words will help and inspire readers.

Keep these thoughts in mind, particularly when you feel lost or are unsure: "My purpose is about giving. I'll direct my thoughts off of me, and spend the next few hours looking for a way to be of service to anyone or any creature on our endangered planet." This will bring you back to a realization that it doesn't matter what you do, as long as you're able to give.

Reflect on your goals for your life. How can you frame each one as a way of being in service to others?

FEELING CONNECTED MEANS YOU TRULY SENSE THAT WE ARE ALL ONE, AND THAT HARM DIRECTED AT OTHERS IS REALLY HARM DIRECTED AT OURSELVES.

Here, cooperation supplants competition; hatred is dissolved with love; and sadness is reduced to nothingness with joy. At this level, you're a member of the human race, not a sub-group. Here, you're a nation of the world with a global awareness, rather than a patriot of any one country. In mystical consciousness, you won't feel separate from anyone, anything, or God. You won't be what you *have*, what you *accomplish*, or what others *think* of you. You will be the beloved, and you will have changed your mind! Problems will now be only illusions of the mind that you no longer carry around with you.

As I look back at many of the decisions I made that took me down my life's path, it's clear that I was making those decisions exclusively on the basis of what felt right, what made me feel passionate and enthusiastic, even when the potential for failure and disappointment was a real possibility.

See your own life more clearly today—right here, right now in this moment—by refusing to ignore that which stirs passion and excitement within you. You came here with music to play, so when you begin to harmonize with what only you hear playing in your mind, listen carefully and stop yourself right in your tracks and be willing to take the first step in the direction of those synchronistic callings. This is your highest self calling! This is your reemergence with your Source of being.

It may not make any sense to anyone around you, and might even appear to be preposterous to you as well, but just know that in the end you will not be disappointed. In fact, whoever and whatever you need will eventually appear in their unforeseen Divine perfection. Even if nothing seems to be going right and it all looks like doom and gloom, stay with your excitement. Declare yourself to be in a state of faith and trust, meditate on your vision, and the support will ultimately be forthcoming. The reason that it serves your inner excitement is because in those moments, known only to you, you are in alignment with who you truly are.

Returning to the list you made at the beginning of the journal, has it changed? Do you hear a clear message from your soul now? What steps will you take to bring your vision into reality? How will you live your purpose? Write or draw on the following pages. You may also want to use these pages for additional expression on any of the journal's exercises, or for what has come up for you as you've been reading. May you feel the miracle of your life!

ABOUT THE AUTHOR

Affectionately called the "father of motivation" by his fans, **Dr. Wayne W. Dyer** was an internationally renowned author, speaker, and pioneer in the field of self-development. Over the four decades of his career, he wrote more than 40 books (21 of which became *New York Times* bestsellers), created numerous audio programs and videos, and appeared on thousands of television and radio shows. His books *Manifest Your Destiny*, *Wisdom of the Ages*, *There's a Spiritual Solution to Every Problem*, and the *New York Times* bestsellers *10 Secrets for Success and Inner Peace*, *The Power of Intention*, *Inspiration*, *Change Your Thoughts—Change Your Life*, *Excuses Begone!*, *Wishes Fulfilled*, and *I Can See Clearly Now* were all featured as National Public Television specials.

Wayne held a doctorate in educational counseling from Wayne State University, had been an associate professor at St. John's University in New York, and honored a lifetime commitment to learning and finding the Higher Self. In 2015, he left his body, returning to Infinite Source to embark on his next adventure.

Website: www.DrWayneDyer.com